THE SCOTTSBORO BOYS TRIAL

A Primary Source Account

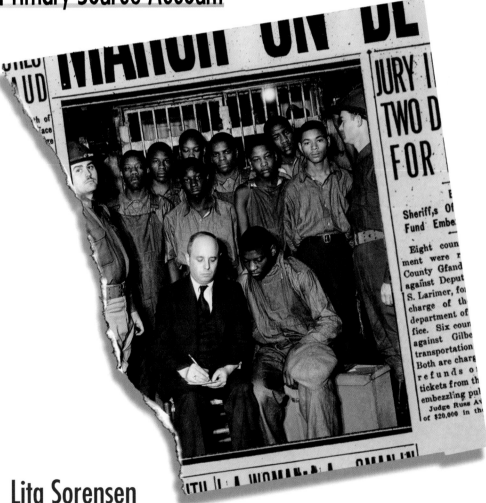

Lita Sorensen

rosen central
Primary Source™
The Rosen Publishing Group, Inc., New York

For my father, James M. Sorensen

Published in 2004 by The Rosen Publishing Group, Inc.
29 East 21st Street, New York, NY 10010

Unless otherwise attributed, all quotes in this book are excerpted from court transcripts.

Library of Congress Cataloging-in-Publication Data
Sorensen, Lita.
The Scottsboro Boys Trial: a primary source account/by Lita Sorensen.—1st ed.
    p. cm.—(Great trials of the twentieth century)
Includes bibliographical references and index.
ISBN 0-8239-3975-8 (library binding)
1. Scottsboro Trial, Scottsboro, Ala., 1931. 2. Trials (Rape)—Alabama—Scottsboro. [1. African Americans—Civil rights—History.]
I. Title. II. Series: Great trials of the 20th century.
KF224.S34 S67 2003
345.761'9502532—dc21

2002153356

Manufactured in the United States of America

CONTENTS

82 547

This photo, taken on March 25, 1931, outside the Scottsboro, Alabama, jail shows the black teenagers who would become known as the Scottsboro Boys. From left to right: Clarence Norris, Olen Montgomery, Andy Wright, Willie Roberson, Ozie Powell, Eugene Williams, Charlie Weems, Roy Wright, and Haywood Patterson. After they were falsely accused of gang rape by two white women, their case would become one of the most controversial and complicated in American history.

INTRODUCTION

The story of the Scottsboro Boys begins when a freight train heading west toward Memphis, Tennessee, stops in Paint Rock, Alabama, and nine black young men, ranging in age from twelve to twenty, are arrested for the rape of two white girls.

It is March 25, 1931, right in the middle of the Great Depression, and thousands of people across the nation are unemployed, hungry, restless, and bored. Many have taken to riding freight trains in order to search for work in neighboring towns and states.

On this particular train on the Southern Railroad Line, a fight breaks out among the two dozen or so mostly young passengers squabbling for space in the railroad cars. A white teenager steps on the hand of a black teenager named Haywood Patterson. The white boy refuses to apologize or admit to being wrong, and a stone throwing fight begins. The black gang outnumbers the white gang, and eventually the whites are forced off the train.

About forty miles down the tracks, the train stops in the town of Paint Rock. None of the black boys involved in the fight considers that strange, as the train had been stopping about every hour along the way.

A few of them look out of the freight cars to see what town they are in. What they see are dozens of white men with rifles and pistols—an armed posse—rushing in to grab Haywood Patterson, his friends, and any other black boys they can find in the cars. The captured boys are marched into a line, tied to each other in a truck, and taken to jail in Scottsboro, Alabama. The white boys who were forced off the train had made up a story that a black gang had assaulted them, and the stationmaster had wired ahead to the next town, Scottsboro.

Also among the freight train riders stopped in Paint Rock are two poor, young, white, female mill workers. They had also jumped the train, hoping to find work. The posse of men questions the girls and prompts them to say that a gang of black boys, the very ones in custody, had raped them.

At this point, the state of Alabama is proud that the posse has not turned into a lynch mob. The governor, B. M. Miller, orders the National Guard onto the scene to protect the accused. However, even before the trial starts, some local newspapers decide that the young men are guilty. A headline from the *Jackson County Sentinel* of March 25, 1931, reads, "All Negroes Positively Identified By Girls And One White Boy Who Was Held Prisoner With Pistol and Knives While Nine Black Fiends Committed Revolting Crime."

And this is how it began.

The controversy of the Scottsboro Boys case was to last over a decade and produce accusations, unfairness, and countless trials and retrials, more than any case in American history. Once again, America was divided on the issue of racial injustice. Although this case made strides in that it allowed southern blacks to serve on court-appointed juries, it consumed the lives of nine young black men who were accused of a crime they did not commit.

A JOURNEY INTERRUPTED

O f the Scottsboro Boys accused of rape, five were from various parts of Georgia and four were from Tennessee. Haywood Patterson, eighteen, of Elberton, Georgia, was traveling with his friend Eugene Williams, thirteen, of Chattanooga, Tennessee. Joining them were two brothers also from Chattanooga—twelve-year-old Roy Wright and nineteen-year-old Andy Wright.

Clarence Norris, nineteen, the son of a former slave, was looking for work on the railroad line and didn't know any of the other eight Scottsboro Boys. Charlie Weems, twenty, from Chattanooga, Tennessee, also didn't know any of the other boys. Olen Montgomery and Ozie Powell, both seventeen and from rural Georgia, and sixteen-year-old Willie Roberson of Columbus, Georgia, did not know each other or any of the other boys when they were arrested.

Most of the boys' backgrounds were similar. All were very poor. Most could not read or write very well and had little formal education. Later interviewed by the head of the Scottsboro Boys Defense Committee, Dr. Allan K. Chalmers, for his book *They Shall Be Free*, one

THE GREAT DEPRESSION

The Great Depression is considered the worst economic crisis of modern history. It lasted from the end of 1929 until the beginning of the 1940s, with devastating effects on the United States as well as the rest of the world. The stock market crashed, banks and businesses closed, and people lost their jobs and homes. Millions of people were unemployed as a direct result of the crisis.

Life during the Depression took a heavy toll on people from varied walks of life. Many lacked enough food to eat, a permanent place to live, and adequate clothing. Some teenagers were able to find jobs when their parents could not. They became the "breadwinners" who supported their parents and other members of the family.

The black community suffered more than other groups because they had a harder time finding and keeping jobs. Employers had a prejudicial preference for white workers, and blacks were the last hired and the first to be let go. Almost half of the United States's black population was unemployed during some years of the Great Depression.

of the boys said, "I could have been something . . . but I just didn't go to school when I should. I played hooky. I fooled my mother. When she thought I was in school I was just playing around."

Several of the boys had quit school to help earn money to support their parents and siblings. Dr. Chalmers, however, was careful to point out in his book that the boys' lives were much like the lives of most black teenagers who lived through the Depression years. The tragedy was that most young black men's lives were so similar.

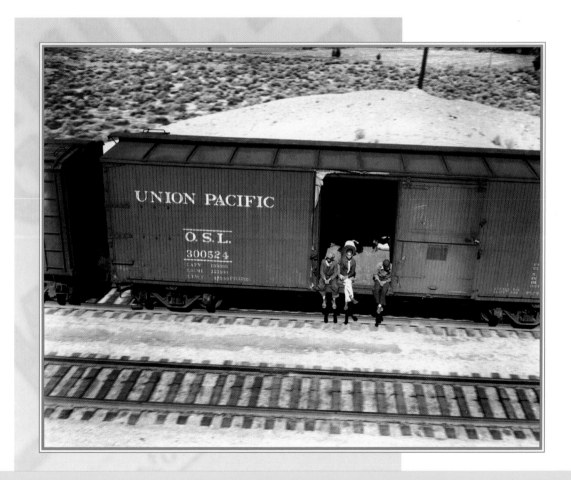

"Hoboing," or jumping freight trains in order to seek work or adventure in other towns or states, was a common activity in some areas of the United States during the Depression. This photo, taken in California on October 23, 1934, shows several hobos hanging over the side of a freight car as the train rushes south. For some people, this method of travel was the only affordable escape from lives marked by poverty and despair.

At least two of the boys, Willie Roberson and Olen Montgomery, were traveling on the Southern Railroad Line to seek medical assistance for disabling conditions. Roberson, who was infected with both syphilis and gonorrhea (two sexually transmitted diseases), could barely walk and was looking for free medical care. Montgomery was extremely nearsighted and had a cataract in one eye. He was looking for a job on the rails to buy a new pair of eyeglasses for himself.

Victoria Price, pictured in the Morgan County Courthouse in Decatur, Alabama, on April 1, 1933. A heavy drinker of questionable character, Price was described during the trials as "a common street prostitute of the lowest type" who had been overheard asking "negro men" about the size of their "private parts."

THE ACCUSERS

Victoria Price, twenty-one, and Ruby Bates, seventeen, the two young white women who accused the Scottsboro Boys of raping them, were also hoboing aboard the Southern Railroad Line when it was stopped by the armed posse in Paint Rock, Alabama. Although they had very different personalities, both girls had a similar social and economic background.

Both girls lived with their mothers in unpainted shacks and supported their families. Victoria Price was a mill worker in her hometown of Huntsville, Alabama. When there wasn't any work for her or Ruby Bates in town, they took to traveling by rail cars in search of work in neighboring towns and states. There were rumors that Price made extra money from prostitution and that she often had black men as clients.

Ruby Bates was the quieter of the two girls, and she let Victoria Price do most of the talking when questioned by the armed posse and by the authorities. She, too, had grown up poor, in a part of town where blacks and whites lived together, worked together, and socialized on an equal basis. It was whispered that she had once been arrested for hugging a black man in public.

Although neither girl had much education, both were familiar with the phrases "white supremacy" and "segregation." They knew that "respectable" people in the segregated South considered them as low class as any white women could be, as they lived in the worst parts of town and associated, worked with, and dated blacks.

Ruby Bates, photographed during interviews by the Scottsboro Boys' attorneys on May 3, 1933, in New York City. Months after the first trial, Bates, who had written a letter to her boyfriend stating, "Those Negroes did not touch me or those white boys. [I] hope you will believe me the law don't," took back her accusation.

That all changed when they said they had been raped. It was unclear whether the girls had been the first to suggest rape, or if the armed posse had suggested it when the girls were first taken off the train with the nine black boys. What is evident is that both Victoria Price and Ruby Bates knew that they had not been raped, nor had they been hurt in any other way by the boys. It may be that both girls wanted the attention they had never had in their lives. Becoming victims would be their chance to be seen for once as virtuous southern white women. Viewed as victims, they would be raised to a new status in society.

THE STORY OF TWO WHITE GIRLS

From the very beginning, the story of a brutal rape caused a whirlwind of talk throughout the state of Alabama. By the evening of March 25, 1931, the entire state was aware of the reported facts, as were other states across the country.

Victoria Price and Ruby Bates gave interviews to newspapers the day after they said the rapes took place. The girls told newspapers that they had been returning to their hometown, where they had caught a freight train earlier to look for work in the cotton mills of neighboring towns. They had become cold after riding on the side of a rail car and so they had switched to a coal car. There they were joined by seven white boys.

Then, very quickly, they said, twelve black teenagers had jumped into their car, waving knives and guns, and forced the white boys off the train. After that, the women said that they were held down, their clothes were ripped off, and knives were held to their throats while the black boys repeatedly raped them.

The South had never heard of such an awful crime.

On April 4, 1933, in Decatur, Alabama, main witness Victoria Price testifies against Haywood Patterson, the first of the nine Scottsboro Boys to stand trial. The *New York Times* noted of Price's performance, "Her direct examination took just twelve minutes of the court's time. When it was finished she settled back in her chair, crossed her silk-stockinged legs and met a day-long attack upon her character and credibility with angry defiance."

At the jail, Victoria Price pointed to six of the nine boys, indicating they were the ones who had raped her. According to Douglas O. Linder's "The Trials of The Scottsboro Boys" Web page, a guard at the jail replied, "If those six had Miss Price, it stands to reason that the others had Miss Bates."

Reportedly, one of the accused boys, Clarence Norris, called out that the girls were liars and was hit with a bayonet. Outside, an angry mob gathered at the jail, calling for Old Southern Justice, better known as a lynching. As a result of Governor Miller's intervention, this never occurred.

The courthouse in Scottsboro, Alabama, as it appeared on April 4, 1933. Roy Wright, one of the accused, was tried in this building on April 7, 1931. While awaiting trail, he wrote to his mother from Blair County Jail, "While in my cell, lonely and thinking of you . . . If you please, send me some paper and stamps so I can write more often."

THE PUBLIC AND THE PROSECUTION

There were only twelve days between the arrests of the Scottsboro Boys and the time they appeared in the courtroom of Judge A. E. Hawkins of Jackson County. The prosecution had decided to try the boys in groups of two or three instead of trying all of them at once. Trying all the boys at once would have been improper legal procedure. The prosecution didn't want to risk the judge ruling a mistrial.

Some local citizens were upset about what they saw as a delay in the indictment of the boys. But Judge Hawkins was able to persuade most people that rushing the proceedings

SOUTHERN RACIAL INJUSTICE AND LYNCHING

E ven into the mid-twentieth century, most black people lived in the southern states. Most were the descendants of slave populations that had been bought and sold to owners of large southern plantations to work in cotton and tobacco fields. Before the Civil War (1861–1865) most white southerners considered black slavery essential and important to the southern way of life.

Even before the Civil War, lynching was common practice in the South. In the beginning, most lynch mob victims were white antislavery activists. After the war, lynching became a tool used mainly against blacks. Despite laws that required fairness and justice, blacks were often lynched when accused of crimes against whites. Even as late as the 1960s, supporters of black civil rights in the South were killed by lynch mobs.

would be seen as a "legal lynching." Newspaper editorials urged that court procedures be followed in punishing the boys, so people in other regions of the country could not accuse the South of being unjust. But, as the *Jackson County Sentinel* put it, ". . . the case against the negroes appears to be the most revolting in the criminal records of our state, and certainly our country." Over weeks and months, this running newspaper commentary summed up the basic feeling of most in the South. Most local white people wanted a swift punishment for the atrocious crime. They did not want a fair trial where the accused were presumed innocent before proven guilty.

Indeed, a fair trial under such circumstances was practically impossible. The newspapers and public sentiment had already found the nine Scottsboro Boys guilty and sentenced them to death.

THE ROLE OF THE NEWSPAPERS IN THE TRIAL

Scottsboro had two weekly newspapers, the *Jackson County Sentinel* and the *Scottsboro Progressive Age*. These were the headlines from the *Jackson County Sentinel* on the day the Scottsboro Boys were seized and thrown into jail:

NINE NEGRO MEN RAPE TWO WHITE GIRLS
THREW WHITE BOYS FROM FREIGHT TRAIN AND
HELD WHITE GIRLS PRISONER UNTIL
CAPTURED BY POSSE

ALL NEGROES POSITIVELY IDENTIFIED BY GIRLS
AND ONE WHITE BOY WHO WAS HELD PRISONER
WITH PISTOLS AND KNIVES WHILE NINE BLACK
FIENDS COMMITTED REVOLTING CRIME

These newspapers, which reached a mostly white audience, wrote about the girls and the Scottsboro Boys quite differently. The girls were described only as hardworking young women who supported their poor families. Many newspapers said the boys were "the worst negro characters in Chattanooga." J. Glenn Jordan, a reporter for the *Huntsville Times*, the girls' hometown newspaper, said that while he interviewed the girls, he could hear the blacks in their cells, telling "nasty jokes, unafraid, denying to outsiders that they were guilty, laughing, laughing, joking, joking, unafraid of consequences." Jordan further called the boys "beasts unfit to be called human."

These unbalanced and biased (showing a preference) reports were repeated in newspaper after newspaper. They were picked up by the Associated Press news service wire, which printed them as fact all over the South.

A COURT IN THE OLD SOUTH

On the morning of April 6, 1931, during the opening of the trial for the first group of Scottsboro Boys, the courtroom was crowded and intense with excitement. Three National Guardsmen and thirty enlisted men guarded the entranceway. The town of Scottsboro took on a carnival-like atmosphere. Farmers from the surrounding countryside—accustomed to traveling to Scottsboro on the first Monday of the month to witness the county court trials, which they called Fair Day, now filled the streets of the town in a record turnout. People arrived from all over Alabama and from as far away as Tennessee.

By 7 AM, thousands of people were trying to gain admittance to the trial, seeking permission from the line of National Guard officers and soldiers assembled at the entrance of the courtroom with machine guns. Judge Hawkins ordered the crowd to stay one hundred feet from the courthouse. Many citizens climbed on roofs to get a better view of the spectacle. That day, business in Scottsboro was excellent.

On April 6, 1931, the opening day of the trials, an estimated 10,000 onlookers jammed the courthouse square in Scottsboro. Bayonet-wielding National Guardsmen patrolled the grounds and kept the crowds in order. Women and children were banned from inside the tension-filled courthouse, where the nine Scottsboro Boys awaited trail.

In truth, there was not much to see inside. Judge Hawkins made sure that counsel was provided for the accused boys. Defending the boys would be Stephen Roddy and Milo Moody. Moody was a local member of the bar who would celebrate his seventieth birthday in two months. It was acknowledged by everyone that he was somewhat forgetful, if not yet senile. He had not had a real, paying court case in years. His main interest in acting as an attorney in this case was that he would be paid a fee, even though it would be small.

Stephen Roddy was unpaid, however, and had been retained by a well-respected black doctor, Dr. P. A. Stephens of Chattanooga, who sought to help the Scottsboro Boys. Roddy was not experienced in criminal trials. He was a real-estate attorney who was unprepared and hesitant to take the case. It was reported that he had been charged with public drunkenness and jailed in the past year.

From the beginning, the way that Moody and Roddy conducted their defense showed that they were incompetent. Roddy refused to clarify that he was acting as the boys' attorney. He told the court that he was unfamiliar with Alabama law and that, ". . . If I was paid down here and employed it would be a different thing," according to Dan T. Carter in his book, *Scottsboro, A Tragedy of the American South*. Moody then stepped forward and announced that he was willing to help Roddy with the defense.

And so, with no preparation except a half-hour interview with their inadequate lawyers, the Scottsboro Boys were put on trial.

THE DEFENSE

Following the court's procedure, the boys were tried in small groups, with Clarence Norris and Charley Weems standing trial first. Roddy opened by requesting the trial be moved to a different location. He suggested that a fair and impartial trial for the boys was

In the photo on the left, taken April 10, 1933, Charlie Weems awaits trial in Decatur, Alabama. In the 1938 photo on the right, Clarence Norris sits in an Alabama prison. Norris and Haywood Patterson were tried and sentenced to death in the fall of 1933.

impossible, given the biased newspaper coverage and the use of soldiers to calm the crowds. Lawyers for the prosecution easily dismissed this argument since Roddy could not produce any witnesses to support the claims as true. Those he did put on the stand, Sheriff M. L. Wann of Jackson County and Major Joe Starnes of the United States National Guard, proved stubborn and uncooperative. Both stated that the crowds were not that bad and that the large number of soldiers guarding the courtroom was really not necessary. There was no surprise when Judge Hawkins overruled (denied) the half-hearted request for a change of venue.

Six of the nine boys (Andy Wright, Willie Roberson, Charles Weems, Ozie Powell, Olen Montgomery, and Eugene Williams) had pleaded not guilty and denied raping or even having seen the two white girls. The remaining three said they had witnessed the other defendants raping the girls. Later, they claimed they had done so because of threats and beatings by prison guards and other officials.

When Victoria Price was called forth as a witness, she wore a new dress for the trial. Her account of the "rape" was colorful. She was not at all a shy personality. In recorded testimony before the court and the all-white, all-male jury, she related tidbits that tantalized the crowd. She testified that between taking turns in raping her, her attackers "would not even let me up to spit." Although she had begged them to quit, she said the boys had only replied that they would take her and Ruby up North and "make us their women."

The defense's cross-examination of Victoria Price was only a few minutes in length, and whenever Roddy attempted to suggest that Price was of less than virtuous character, he was stopped short by objections from the prosecution that Judge Hawkins sustained (allowed).

Ozie Powell testifies during a retrial in the courthouse in Decatur, Alabama, on April 7, 1933. Meanwhile, news of the injustice shown during the Scottsboro trials had spread like wildfire across the country. In New York City, a peaceful protest of the Scottsboro verdict turned into a riot.

A SCOTTSBORO BOY'S SAMPLE CASE HISTORY

I left home in Molina, Georgia, in the early teens because I just got to the place where I didn't like my father. He was telling me things that was right and I figured he was wrong and now since I have growed up I realize he was right. I stayed away from him for about two years before going back. I remained home about three months then I went back to Atlanta in 1931 and went to Chattanooga. I stayed in Chattanooga about three days and went back to Atlanta on a passenger train. The last time I left Atlanta in 1931 when I got in trouble I went to Chattanooga, hoboed and stayed one day. I was hoboing my ways to Memphis looking for a job. I had a job in Atlanta working at the slaughter pen and they cut me off and I started pushing the mail wagons at the terminal station and they cut me off from there and that is when I started hoboing.

—From *They Shall Be Free* by Dr. Allan K. Chalmers

THE PROSECUTION

The state, represented by prosecutor H. G. Bailey, called Dr. R. R. Bridges to the stand. Bridges was one of the two doctors who had examined the girls shortly after the alleged rape. The most important thing Bridges revealed was that both girls had had sexual intercourse

Dr. R. R. Bridges, a Scottsboro physician since 1914, testified in the first retrial on April 3, 1933. He and his assistant, Dr. John Lynch, examined Victoria Price and Ruby Bates after the young women had cried rape. Bridges noted that neither of the two women (whom he examined less than two hours after the alleged assault) "was hysterical, or nervous about [the examination] at all." Their pulse rates were normal and their breathing was not labored. More important, the sperm found inside them was too old to have come from a recent rape.

sometime before his examination. But as to Victoria Price's story of violence and being held down roughly, there was no evidence. There were no serious bruises or cuts anywhere on the girls' bodies. Nevertheless, the doctor did assert that it was still quite possible, in his expert opinion, that six men could indeed have gang-raped Victoria Price without causing her the physical damage usually associated with rape. Dr. Bridges's testimony greatly helped the prosecution's side.

Due mainly to more objections by the prosecution, defense lawyers Roddy and Moody did not get to cross-examine the doctor about his testimony at all.

When Ruby Bates took the stand, she was quieter and more hesitant to tell the events that took place concerning the rape. More important, her story differed significantly from that of her friend. Incredibly, Roddy did not even mention this in his cross-examination.

A guilty verdict for the first group of boys, Clarence Norris and Charley Weems, was swift. When the jury announced the decision, the large crowd gathered outside let out a loud shout of approval, which could be heard clearly by the jury at the trial for the second group.

The trials lasted from April 6 through April 9. The boys were used as witnesses for and against each other. More testimony was heard from Victoria Price and Dr. Bridges. Other witnesses were introduced. When the trials (four in all) for each group were over, all the Scottsboro Boys were sentenced to die in the electric chair, except for twelve-year-old Roy Wright, who, because of his age, had been sentenced to life in prison.

THE ROLE OF THE NAACP AND THE ILD

U nexpectedly, a swell of protest against the unfair proceedings at Scottsboro came from all over the country. People from all walks of life wrote to the Alabama governor's office on behalf of the boys. Most letters came from the North, but some came from the South, too. They came from black maids in New York City; white lawyers in Atlanta, Georgia; artists, poets, clergymen, school teachers, and many others.

There had been quite a few cases similar to the Scottsboro Boys trials (unfair rape cases involving black men) in recent years that had gone unnoticed. These trials were different, however. Because of the boys' ages, the obvious speed and unfairness of the trials, and the severity of the punishment, the world had taken notice of them.

Although many thought that the National Association for the Advancement of Colored People (NAACP) would be the primary group to organize a fight to save the Scottsboro Boys, it did not happen. The NAACP had worked hard in previous years to build a respectable reputation in support of black causes. The issue of a black man raping a white woman was so taboo (forbidden) that the NAACP was reluctant to step forward in case any of the boys were actually found guilty of committing the crime.

Instead, it was the American Communist Party that took the first step. The boys' execution was scheduled for July 10, 1931. On April 9, the International Labor Defense (ILD), a legal organization and part of the Communist Party in the United States, sent a statement to the Alabama governor's office demanding a stay of execution (a postponement) in the Scottsboro case. The ILD also wanted to be able to investigate and prepare for an appeal.

Members of the ILD approached the boys in prison. They also talked to people who wanted to help the boys, such as the Chattanooga Negro Ministers' Alliance. The ILD's chief attorney, Joseph Brodsky, promised

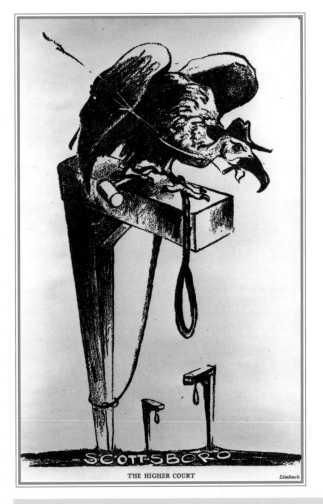

THE HIGHER COURT   Limbach

This political cartoon, entitled "The Higher Court," was drawn in 1931. The greedy vulture with the gavel represents the higher court, ready to swoop down on the Scottsboro Boys and hang them. Judged to be motivated by racism, the trials were gaining a following of people who were outraged at the unfairness of the proposed death sentences.

that in the next trial, the Scottsboro Boys would have the best lawyers in the country, along with the support of members of the Communist Party all over the country.

The
SCOTTSBORO BOYS
MUST NOT DIE!

MASS SCOTTSBORO DEFENSE MEETING

At St. Mark's M. E. Church
137th Street and St. Nicholas Avenue

Friday Eve., April 14th, 8 P. M.

Protest the infamous death verdict rendered by an all-white jury at Decatur, Alabama against HAYWOOD PATTERSON

The Meeting will be addressed by:

Mrs. JANIE PATTERSON, mother of Haywood Patterson, victim of the lynch verdict; SAMUEL LEIBOWITZ, chief counsel for the defense; JOSEPH BRODSKY, defense counsel; WILLIAM PATTERSON, National Secretary of the I. L. D.; RICHARD B. MOORE; Dr. LORENZO KING; WM. KELLEY of the Amsterdam News; and others.

THUNDER YOUR INDIGNATION AGAINST THE JUDICIAL MURDER OF INNOCENT NEGRO CHILDREN!

COME TO THE MASS PROTEST MEETING

AT ST. MARK'S M. E. CHURCH
137th Street and St. Nicholas Avenue

FRIDAY EVENING, APRIL 14th, 8 P. M.

Emergency Scottsboro Defense Committee
119 West 135th Street, New York City

Printed in 1931 by members of the Emergency Scottsboro Defense Committee, this poster reflects the outrage felt by some Americans with regards to the Scottsboro Boys' guilty verdicts. Many people rallied together to gather support for Haywood Patterson and the other prisoners. Their hope was to put a stop to Patterson's execution.

He asked the boys to sign an affidavit turning the case over to the ILD. Everything Brodsky presented sounded favorable, so the imprisoned young men eagerly signed.

THE NAACP ENTERS

Support from the NAACP was offered too late. Walter White, the director of the NAACP, urged the boys not to sign anything and not to commit themselves in any way to the ILD. Members of the Chattanooga Negro Ministers' Alliance were furnished with more information about the ILD. Concerned about the Communist Party's motives in defending the case, the ministers had legal documents drawn up for the Scottsboro Boys to sign again, stating that they did not wish the ILD to help them.

By this time, needless to say, the young men were completely confused. They signed their names again when the ministers asked them to.

But the ILD was still determined to champion the case. They found support among the parents and relatives of the boys. They urged the parents to send letters in support of their organization to their children in prison. To make sure that the boys signed over to the ILD once again, the parents were brought to the jail in a special car. This was the first time that the parents had seen their sons since they had been arrested. There were tears of gladness, and in no time the boys had signed back to the ILD.

Another tactic of the ILD was to attack and discredit the NAACP. This was done through demonstrations and through written and spoken slogans. The NAACP was accused of being afraid of the white power structure and accepting conditions that had become status quo for blacks.

In the end, after much fighting to gain the support of the boys and the support of popular opinion, the NAACP lost out to the ILD. For many reasons, among them its failure to win over the black

THE SCOTTSBORO BOYS IN JAIL

The living conditions in the prison where the Scottsboro Boys were sent to wait on death row were substandard and inhumane. The boys could hear executions taking place, for their cells were not far from the death chamber. Guards were abusive and tormented the boys.

While in prison, the teenagers talked, feuded with one another, remembered what life was like outside the bars that held them, and thought about girls. They wrote many letters to friends and family on cheap stationery. Some didn't know how to write, so other prisoners would help them out.

In *Stories of Scottsboro*, James Goodman examined the boys' letters. "While in my cell lonely and thinking of you," Roy Wright, then age thirteen, wrote, "I am trying by some means to write a few words. I would like for you come down hear Thursday . . . I feel I can eat some of your cooking Mom."

Ozie Powell wrote his family a lengthy Christmas list. He asked for "1 coconut, 2 nice cakes, chocolate and coconut, 1 pound mixed nuts, 1 doz. Apples, 1 doz. Oranges, 1 doz. Bananas and candy, 3 blocks of grape chewing gum, 2 pairs of socks and some cheese an some fried rabbit and sausage and some fried potato pies. And some sauce meat. And some rexall tooth paste and some stamps envelopes and tablet."

newspapers, failure to win over the boys' parents, and mainly because they had reacted too slowly in the beginning of the trials, the NAACP was eventually forced to withdraw from the bid to defend the Scottsboro Boys.

The nine young men had cast their lot with the ILD. The court finally issued a stay of execution just seventy-two hours before they were scheduled to die in the electric chair.

APPEALS, OUTCOMES, AND A LANDMARK DECISION

Early in 1932, the ILD filed an appeal with the Alabama Supreme Court, arguing that the boys had been denied a fair trial because the jury had been prejudiced and the defense counsel had been insufficient. The court upheld the previous guilty verdict by a 6-1 vote. It also kept the death penalty in all but one boy's case. According to the court, thirteen-year-old Eugene Williams should not have been tried as an adult.

But the ILD would not give up. It took the case all the way to the United States Supreme Court, where it was heard before nine Supreme Court justices instead of a jury. The ILD had hired Walter Pollack, one of the country's best constitutional lawyers. It was Pollack's argument before the Supreme Court that first stressed the point that the Scottsboro Boys had been denied a fair trial because no blacks had been allowed on the jury. As a matter of fact, blacks had not been allowed on any juries in Jackson County, Alabama, since the Reconstruction period after the Civil War. Pollack also stressed the lack of adequate legal counsel for the boys.

On September 7, 1932, the Supreme Court of Alabama called for a new set of trials for the Scottsboro Boys. The trials were held in this courthouse in Decatur, pictured here on April 4, 1933—eight days after the new trials began. The town of Decatur has a long and interesting history. When the Civil War swept over the South, much of the town was destroyed in battle. When the battle ended in 1864, only four buildings were left standing.

On November 7, 1932, the Supreme Court announced its decision. In a vote of 7 to 2, it ruled that the Scottsboro Boys' rights had been violated under the protection of the Fourteenth Amendment, or the right of every citizen to due process of the law. This decision, known as *Powell v. Alabama*, was heralded as a landmark case (a case having great importance). The decision specified that it was the state's responsibility to see that defendants were provided with adequate legal counsel.

The ILD was hopeful. It told the boys that they would have a new chance at life and that they would all eventually go free.

The Supreme Court decision also called for a new set of trials in Alabama for the Scottsboro Boys. They would be held in Decatur, a town fifty miles away from Scottsboro. This time, at the request of the ILD and the Communist Party, the well-known New York City attorney Samuel Leibowitz was to serve as chief attorney, with ILD attorney Joseph Brodsky to assist.

SECOND ROUND OF TRIALS

The second trial of Haywood Patterson was scheduled for March 30, 1933, with Judge James Horton presiding in the case. Leibowitz opened by arguing for an appeal, based on the fact that blacks had been denied representation on the jury in Jackson County, Alabama. He put black witnesses on the stand to show that they had never been called for jury duty. And although Judge Horton acknowledged the point, he refused to acknowledge that this was grounds for a mistrial.

Victoria Price was put on the stand by the Alabama attorney general, Thomas Knight Jr., who was trying the case. His questions for her were brief. Once again she told her well-documented story of the train ride and her rape by the defendants, adding a few embellishments for her audience, here and there. In her new testimony, she told the jury that while

Victoria Price and her boyfriend, Jack Tiller, are photographed as they walk to the retrial of Haywood Patterson on November 29, 1933, in Decatur, Alabama. The defense testimony suggested that Price had sexual relations with Tiller just days before the supposed rape had occurred, which would explain the dead semen Dr. Bridges discovered in Price during his examination.

she was being raped, her attacker had told her that when he was done, "You will have a black baby," according to Douglas O. Linder's Web site.

But this time, the defense attorney was ready for her. On his cross-examination, he mercilessly questioned her story, attacking her character at the same time. It was known all over that she was a prostitute in her hometown, he suggested, and went by the nickname of "Big Leg Price." She was known to be an adulterer. She had never been raped, he claimed, and was making up the story against the Scottsboro Boys so that she could avoid being thrown in jail for prostitution.

All of Leibowitz's witnesses were chosen to discredit Price. One of the doctors who had examined both Victoria Price and Ruby Bates shortly after the rape reappeared, and upon further questioning by the defense, stated that both girls had remained calm and were not bleeding or damaged when he examined them. Furthermore, the sperm he had found in the girls' vaginas were not alive. This showed it was unlikely that the girls had been raped by the Scottsboro Boys during the time they claimed to have been raped.

On April 7, 1933, "witness" Lester Carter testifies on the stand in the Decatur courtroom in the second trial of Haywood Patterson. Though Victoria Price claimed that she did not know Carter, Ruby Bates later testified otherwise. An excerpt of her testimony stated that "Victoria and Jack and myself and Lester all left and walked up the Pulaski Pike."

Lester Carter, a young white man who was also traveling on the Southern Railroad train at the time, testified that he had met both girls earlier. Price had denied knowing him. Carter said the two girls had stayed at a hobo camp with Carter and with Price's boyfriend, Jack Tiller. There, the two couples had consensual (agreed upon) sex a few days before the alleged rape.

The Scottsboro Boys themselves were called to the witness stand, among them Willie Roberson. He testified that at the time of the alleged rape, he was so sick with syphilis-related symptoms that he could barely walk, and that he was unable to leap from freight car to freight car, as Victoria Price had claimed he did during the attack.

Ruby Bates sits with the mothers of four of the Scottsboro Boys at a rally in New York City's Madison Square Garden on May 1, 1934. From left to right, Mrs. Norris, Mrs. Montgomery, Bates, Mrs. Williams, and Mrs. Powell. The women were attending a May Day communist rally because the American Communist Party was an aggressive supporter of the accused youths.

STAR WITNESS

Probably the most surprising witness for the defense was Ruby Bates. Nobody had heard from the girl for weeks. When she walked in with two armed National Guardsmen to testify on behalf of the Scottsboro Boys, there were audible gasps of disbelief and amazement in the courtroom.

She told the court she had been suffering from a guilty conscience. She said there had never been a rape, and that she had told her story because Victoria Price had urged her to do so, to avoid being thrown in jail on morals charges.

According to Linder's Web site, the trial closed with associate Alabama prosecutor Wade Wright uttering to the jury the racist remark "Alabama justice can't be bought with Jew money from New

Judge James H. Horton hears the testimony of Victoria Price on April 4, 1933. Horton was soft spoken and well liked for his fairness and legal expertise. Tensions were high in the courtroom during the Scottsboro Boys trial, and many people were calling out for the lynching of the accused. Horton called these rabble-rousers "cowardly lynchers" and ordered armed guards into the courtroom to protect the accused.

York!" Although Judge Horton reminded the jury that they were there to try the case, not lawyers or states, the jury entered the courtroom laughing. The jury found the defendant guilty and sentenced him to death.

Ruby Bates returned to New York with attorney Samuel Leibowitz after this trial. She later became one of the Scottsboro Boys' greatest advocates, marching in parades along with the boys' mothers and fathers, and giving speeches begging for justice and mercy.

On April 18, 1933, Judge Horton called for a postponement of the other young men's trials, due to dangerously high tension and publicity. Then, on June 22, 1933, another stunning reversal occurred. Judge Horton announced that he had heard new evidence proving Victoria Price had not been raped in the Southern Railroad car. Much later, it became clear that a young, white southern doctor who had examined and questioned the girls had found absolutely no evidence that they had been raped. He believed the girls had made up the entire story, but had refused to testify about his belief in court for fear of damaging his career in the segregated communities of Alabama. The older judge had listened to the young doctor with sympathy.

Judge Horton lost his judgeship in the following year's elections. His decision to choose justice over his career and the popular, anti-black sentiment that predominated during the time was a decision that took courage and is to be commended. It is also proof that it takes great strength to stand up against an unjust majority, and that there are those who listen to their consciences and do the right thing when it is important to do so.

THE LONG ROAD TO JUSTICE

After the announcement that there was new evidence to be heard, a third round of trials was in order. Haywood Patterson and Clarence Norris would stand trial. In November 1933, the Scottsboro Boys case was brought before Judge William Callahan. Callahan banned cameras from the courtroom and refused National Guard protection for the defendants. He was a judge who was looking for a no-nonsense, speedy decision in these cases in order to get the Scottsboro Boys and Alabama out of America's newspapers and consciousness. By this time, a rash of violence in the form of lynchings had broken out across the South.

Guilty verdicts were quickly returned. This judge wanted the whole matter finished and over with, and he set a goal of three days to finish all the trials. The boys had been found guilty already, and Judge Callahan thought they were guilty. In fact, Judge Callahan "forgot" to give the jury a form for acquittal, until he was urged to do so by the prosecution. In a sense, he was not allowing for the possibility that the boys could be judged innocent. If he had failed to provide the form, it may have been

Defense lawyer Samuel Leibowitz *(left)*, pictured at the preliminary trials in the Morgan County Courthouse in Decatur, with Haywood Patterson *(center)* and George Chamlee, another member of the defense counsel. In his summation, Leibowitz told the court, "I shall appeal to your reason as logical, intelligent human beings, determined to give even this poor scrap of colored humanity a fair, square deal."

grounds for a mistrial, since this suggested that the court proceedings were prejudiced against the boys. Callahan's actions reflect the worst kind of institutional bias and injustice.

Death sentences were returned for Haywood Patterson and Clarence Norris. Leibowitz, acting as defense counsel, promised to fight for appeals "to Hell and back," according to Linder's Web site.

BACK TO THE SUPREME COURT

On February 15, 1935, the Scottsboro Boys case was once again before the U.S. Supreme Court. Again, a major issue raised was that Alabama had excluded blacks from the jury, in violation of constitutional rights guaranteed to citizens for equal protection under the law. This time, Leibowitz showed that the jury selection process in Judge Callahan's trial had been tampered with, and the names of black citizens supposedly available for selection had been forged sometime after the trial had already begun.

With looks of disgust on their faces, the Supreme Court justices ruled unanimously in *Norris v. Alabama* that due to unconstitutional jury selection in the state of Alabama, the Scottsboro Boys' convictions were unjust.

The defense prepared for one more trial. However, they hoped that the Supreme Court's decision would convince the state of Alabama that the case was not worth more time or the citizens' tax money. Leibowitz hoped to persuade the citizens of Alabama by putting a local attorney named Clarence Watts in the role of chief defense attorney. Leibowitz directed from the sidelines. The new trial was held on January 6, 1936, once more before Judge Callahan.

In accordance with the Supreme Court ruling, the state allowed blacks to be admitted to the jury pool. But they were denied the opportunity of serving on the jury by the state prosecutors. Once again, the jury returned a guilty verdict, although they had found what they considered to be a compromise. They sentenced the young man on trial, Haywood Patterson, to seventy-five years in prison. This marked the first time in Alabama state history that a black man was not given a death sentence for raping a white woman.

THE TRIALS CONTINUE (ROUNDS FOUR AND FIVE)

At the time of Patterson's conviction in 1936, the Scottsboro Boys had been in prison and on trial for over five years. Both the defense and the prosecution seemed sick of the whole affair. There was talk of further compromise. Allan K. Chalmers led the Scottsboro Boys

INTERNATIONAL LABOR DEFENSE, NATIONAL OFFICE
SCOTTSBORO INCOME AND EXPENDITURES
FOR THE PERIOD OF – APRIL 11, 1931 to AUGUST 31, 1934

INCOME:			Percentages
Through I.L.D.	$47,235.66		
N.A.A.C.P.	3,482.20		
A.C.L.U.	2,713.05		
N.C.D.P.P.	8,394.32		
TOTAL INCOME		$61,825.23	100. %

EXPENDITURES:

Legal, Court, Investigation,& Various Litigation expenses:	Paid by I.L.D.	Paid by Lawyers	Total	
Various Decatur Trial expenses	$1,644.50	$1,325.65	$2,970.15	4.9%
Investigations	4,323.35	5,197.84	9,521.19	15.5%
Stenographic Fees for Trial Reports	259.76	645.24	905.00	1.6%
Protection Payments– Lawyers		861.00	861.00	1.5%
Cost of Court Records & printing of appeals	1,942.70	2,451.10	4,393.80	7.1%
Preparation 1934-appeals, (June – August)	1,150.00		1,150.00	1.8%
Paid to Attorneys for taxis, telegrams, telephones, during trials		1,007.30	1,007.30	1.7%
Hotel Expenses, Railroad fare & various other expenses for lawyers and witnesses	2,050.28	2,294.97	4,345.25	7.0%
Payments to Lawyers: Fees & General Expenses	------------	------------	13,027.36	21.0%
Total Legal, Court Investigation, etc.			$38,181.05	62.1%

Other Scottsboro Expenses:			
Prisoners & Parents Relief	3,156.40		5.1%
Parents Fare to Kilby	237.00		0.3%
Mothers Fares	240.12		0.3%
Total		3,633.52	5.7%

Mass Campaigns:			
Mats and Photos	295.03		0.4%
Buttons & Penny Stamps	732.21		1.1%
Mailing & Advertising	819.46		1.3%
Richard B.Moore Tour	173.28		0.3%
Ada Wright "	311.20		0.5%
Engdahl-Wright "	231.68		0.4%
Convention	60.00		0.1%
Org. & Traveling Expenses	1,371.64		2.2%
Scottsboro March to Washington	1,403.59		2.3%
Labor Defender – Advertising	100.00		0.2%
Petitions	51.16		0.1%
Publicity & Publications	2,121.11		3.4%
Total		7,670.36	12.3%

Administrative:			
Telephone & Telegrams	1,858.01		3.0%
Rent	523.35		0.8%
Southern Office	926.57		1.5%
Wages and Subsidies	3,492.81		5.6%
Stationery & Printing	3,112.39		5.1%
Postage	2,869.37		4.6%
Miscellaneous	2,084.42		3.4%
Total		14,866.82	24.0%

TOTAL EXPENDITURES		$64,351.75	104.1%
Due from Scottsboro Campaign		$ 2,526.52	4.1%

We have examined the books and records of the International Labor Defense, National Office, with respect to the Scottsboro Division. We certify, that the above statement correctly reflects the financial transactions for the period.

CENTRAL AUDIT BUREAU

Morris A Greenbaum

BY: M. Greenbaum

This document, housed in the Chicago Historical Society and created by the International Labor Defense national office, lists the fees incurred in the defense of the Scottsboro Boys for the period of April 11, 1931 to August 31, 1934. Note the many expenses, including the defense attorneys' salaries, transportation fees (train tickets, meals, and lodging), expenses for marches and protests to raise awareness of the injustice of the trials, and wages for court reporters.

Defense Committee, which was started in December of 1935. Several organizations, including the American Civil Liberties Union (ACLU), the NAACP, and the ILD finally joined together in support of the Scottsboro Boys. Chalmers was a pastor and a civil rights leader who had great skill as a mediator (negotiator). He was someone able to win over the confidences of most people, even those who were ideologically opposed to him. He worked for understanding among Alabama citizens of the real issues in the case and urged justice.

The state pressed on with its prosecutions, intent on finding the Scottsboro Boys guilty. At this time, seven of the nine young men had been held in prison without trials. A new trial was scheduled for July 12, 1937. Clarence Norris would stand before Judge Callahan. Callahan tried to rush the cases even more because of a stifling atmosphere in courtroom due to the 100-degree Alabama summer heat. This time, during short, consecutive trials, Clarence Norris, Andy Wright, and Charlie Weems were found guilty.

Ozie Powell's rape charges were dropped when he pled guilty to assaulting a deputy with a knife during an escape attempt. While the boys were being transported from jail one day, Powell, still in handcuffs, had grabbed a small knife out of a pocket and stabbed a deputy sheriff in the neck. The sheriff, who was driving, immediately pulled over to the side of a road and shot Powell in the head.

Powell was brain damaged after recovering from the wound. He was sentenced to twenty years for the assault, which was a crime more easily proven than the rape accusations that had been disputed for years by now. Now the prosecution could guarantee that Powell would spend a long time in prison.

THE BOYS FINALLY GO FREE

Then came the big surprise, and perhaps the compromise, too. The state prosecutors announced that charges were dropped against the

Judge Callahan:—"I Instruct You to Bring in a Verdict in Accordance With the Laws of Alabama!"
Jury:—"We Git You, Judge"
—By Burck

Judge Callahan

Scottsboro Jury

Burck

This cartoon by artist Jacob Burck, now housed in the Chicago Historical Society, was printed in the *Daily Worker* on December 1, 1933. The drawing shows Judge Callahan instructing a jury of lynch-happy white jurors who seem eager to shoot, hang, and wreak havoc at any moment. The artist suggests that the Scottsboro Boys trial was merely a formality, and that the law was used to enforce southern racism.

remaining young men, Olen Montgomery, Eugene Williams, Roy Wright, and Willie Roberson. The prosecution said they had become convinced that these boys were innocent of the crime, and that given the other two boys' ages, twelve and thirteen at the time of the rape, they should all be released.

New York City attorney Leibowitz, still active in the case, had the four boys escorted by a special car to the Tennessee border, where

On July 26, 1937, the four Scottsboro Boys who had been freed arrive at Pennsylvania Station in New York City, where they are greeted by a roaring crowd of ecstatic supporters. From left to right stand Eugene Williams, Olen Montgomery, attorney Samuel Leibowitz, Willie Roberson, and Roy Wright. The four boys' journey to freedom took six years.

they were set free. The other boys, still imprisoned, believed that this freedom had been bought with their lives—that this had been the compromise. They were bitter. And although many were sure that the remaining boys would be offered a pardon by the Alabama governor in 1938, this never occurred.

One by one through the years, the Scottsboro Boys left Alabama prisons, either through parole or escapes. Haywood Patterson escaped dramatically in 1948. He wrote a book about his life while he was still being hunted as a prisoner. Shortly after his book was published, he was arrested in Michigan, but the governor refused to send Patterson back to Alabama. Patterson died of cancer at the age of thirty-nine. In 1950, Andy Wright became the last Scottsboro Boy to leave the Alabama state prison system on parole.

THE IMPACT OF THE SCOTTSBORO BOYS TRIAL

Although they became celebrities during the years of the trials, the Scottsboro Boys and their accusers, Victoria Price and Ruby Bates, faded into the background of American life in the years to come. Although the Scottsboro Boys received additional help through the NAACP and Allan K. Chalmers in adjusting to life outside prison again, the rest of their lives were shadowed by unemployment, bad relationships, and poor health. Many went on to marry and have children of their own. Two of the boys, Haywood Patterson (*Scottsboro Boy*, 1950) and Clarence Norris (*The Last of the Scottsboro Boys*, 1979) wrote books about their lives, prison experiences, and the trials from their own perspectives.

Victoria Price and Ruby Bates resurfaced in 1976 when NBC released a television movie, *Judge Horton and the Scottsboro Boys*. Price filed a civil law suit, claiming that her right to privacy had been violated. The case was dismissed by the court.

The lives of the Scottsboro Boys were eaten up by selfishness. Victoria Price and Ruby Bates's desire to get people's attention got in the way of justice. So did the segregated South's refusal to seek the truth. Many people are to blame for this shameful time in America's past. There were those who did not want to tell the truth because of the fear that they might lose their careers. Others wanted to be famous no matter what the cost. And there were people who let their personal ideas about race take priority over the rights of innocent people.

Probably the most important impact the Scottsboro Boys trial had on American history is that it sparked the start of the black civil rights movement of the 1960s. People from the North and the South, black and white, rallied around the Scottsboro Boys. They fought for justice in the face of racial discrimination. The case paved the way for support of such black civil rights figures as Rosa Parks and Dr. Martin Luther King Jr.

LANDMARK DECISIONS

Through two landmark Supreme Court decisions, the rights of all American citizens were refined and expanded. Especially affected were black citizens in the segregated South, whose civil rights were finally beginning to be recognized by the whole country.

In *Powell v. Alabama*, the Supreme Court further defined the right of all people to competent and, if necessary, state-appointed legal counsel when accused and arrested for a crime.

In 1932, the Court wrote about the Scottsboro Boys that,

" . . . the ignorance and illiteracy of the defendants, their youth, the circumstances of public hostility, the imprisonment and the close surveillance of the defendants by the military forces, the fact that their friends and families were all in other states and communication with them necessarily difficult, and above all that they stood in deadly peril of their lives—we think the failure of the (Alabama) trial court to give them reasonable time and opportunity to secure counsel was a clear denial of due process . . . "

The Court wrote that even when there is no law or statute ordering a court to do so, that under the U.S. Constitution, it is the responsibility of a court to provide an appointed attorney, even if the accused is unable to pay for one, is illiterate, or is unable to understand what is going on.

Patterson v. Alabama and *Norris v. Alabama* expanded the civil rights of blacks in the racially divided South so that they might serve on any court-appointed jury. By its own state law, Alabama was required to place on the jury roll all men considered honest, with "integrity, good character, and sound judgment," who were not under twenty-one years of age and who were not "habitual drunkards."

The Supreme Court wrote in its opinion (1935), "there was abundant evidence that there were a large number of negroes in the county who were qualified for jury service. Men of intelligence, some of whom were college graduates, testified to long lists of such qualified negroes . . ." They went on to say that the Alabama court, because of its racial prejudice, was systematically keeping blacks from serving on juries, and that it would have to change.

The civil rights that were denied the Scottsboro Boys and other blacks in the segregated South are something that we do not think much about these days. Everyone now recognizes that anybody accused of a crime has the right to a lawyer. Everyone knows somebody, black, white, or of any other race, who has been asked to serve on a jury. But in 1931, those rights did not apply to all citizens. It took years of fighting for justice, and in part, the sacrifice of the Scottsboro Boys' young lives, to achieve these rights that we take for granted today.

THE SCOTTSBORO BOYS TIMELINE

March 25, 1931   The Scottsboro Boys are arrested in Paint Rock, Alabama, and accused of raping Victoria Price and Ruby Bates.

March 30, 1931   The Scottsboro Boys are indicted for the crime of raping two white women, a crime that carries the death penalty in Alabama.

April 6, 1931   The Scottsboro Boys' trials begin before Judge A. E. Hawkins

April 7–9, 1931   All the Scottsboro Boys but Roy Wright, because of his age, are found guilty and sentenced to death.

April–December 1931   The NAACP and the ILD fight for legal representation of the boys in court.

June 22, 1931   The Scottsboro Boys are granted a stay of execution.

January 1932   The NAACP officially withdraws, and the ILD, an arm of the Communist Party is set to represent the boys in court.

March 1932   The Alabama Supreme Court affirms the boys' convictions and sentences. Eugene Williams's conviction is reversed because of his age.

November 1932 — In *Powell v. Alabama*, the U.S. Supreme Court reverses previous Alabama court decisions, by finding that Alabama did not provide adequate counsel for the defendants according to the rights listed under the Fourteenth Amendment of the U.S. Constitution.

March 27, 1933 — A new Scottsboro Boys trial begins before Judge James Horton in Decatur, Alabama.

April 9, 1933 — A guilty verdict and death sentence is delivered in Judge Horton's courtroom against Haywood Patterson.

June 22, 1933 — Judge Horton grants a new trial based on new evidence found.

November–December 1933 — In a new trial in Judge William Callahan's court, the boys are found guilty again and sentenced to the electric chair.

June 1934 — The Alabama Supreme Court upholds the guilty verdicts.

April 1, 1935 — The U.S. Supreme Court, in *Norris v. State of Alabama*, finds the guilty verdicts unconstitutional because blacks were denied representation on juries during the trials.

December 1935 — The Scottsboro Boys Defense Committee is formed, with Dr. Allan K. Chalmers leading.

January 23, 1936 Guilty convictions are upheld, but for the first time, the sentence is compromised to seventy-five years in prison for Haywood Patterson. This is the first time any black man has been given less than a sentence of death for raping a white woman in the state of Alabama.

June 14, 1937 Another guilty verdict and conviction upheld by the Alabama Supreme Court.

July 1937 Although there has been talk of compromise, Clarence Norris, Andy Wright, and Charlie Weems are convicted again before Judge Callahan. Ozie Powell's sentence for rape is dropped as he pleads guilty to assaulting a deputy.

July 24, 1937 Charges against Olen Montgomery, Willie Roberson, Eugene Williams, and Roy Wright are dropped. They are set free.

June 1950 Through either escape or parole through the years, the Scottsboro Boys are eventually all free. Andy Wright is the last to leave the Alabama state prison system on parole.

GLOSSARY

acquittal   A judgment where a person is found not guilty of a crime he or she has been charged with.

affidavit   A written statement for use as legal evidence sworn to be true.

alleged   Accused of committing a crime.

appeal   The request for a new trial after an initial court decision.

bayonet   A rifle with a blade attached.

civil rights movement   An organized movement to secure for blacks and other groups the rights, privileges, and protection secured for citizens under the U.S. Constitution.

conviction   The act of showing or declaring a person guilty of a crime.

defense   The attorneys hired or appointed to represent the accused.

indict   To formally charge suspects with a crime.

mistrial   A trial that is invalid because of procedural error.

moral charges   Laws that prohibit crossing state lines for immoral purposes, such as prostitution.

pardon   Cancellation of a crime or punishment by someone with the authority to do so.

parole   Release of a convicted person that is earned by good behavior in prison before his or her sentence has expired.

prejudice   A judgment formed before getting all the facts.

prosecution   The party pressing charges or prosecuting another for a crime.

segregation   The separation of people by race, class, or ethnic group.

status quo   A Latin term meaning the state of affairs as it is now or was before a recent change.

Supreme Court   The highest court in the United States, presided over by nine justices, and having authority over all other courts.

verdict   A decision; in law, the decision reached by a jury.

white supremacy   Belief in the superiority and domination of the white or Caucasian race.

FOR MORE INFORMATION

Alabama Department of Archives and History
624 Washington Avenue
Montgomery, AL 36130-0100
(334) 242-4435
Web site: http://www.archives.state.al.us

American Civil Liberties Union (ACLU)
125 Broad Street, 18th Floor
New York, NY 10004
(212) 549-2585
Web site: http://www.aclu.org

Charles H. Wright Museum of African American History
315 East Warren Avenue
Detroit, MI 48201-1443
(313) 494-5800
Web site: http://www.maah-detroit.org

**National Association for the Advancement of Colored
  People (NAACP)**
4805 Mt. Hope Drive
Baltimore, MD 21215
(877) NAACP-98 (622-2798)
Web site: http://www.naacp.org

WEB SITES

Due to the changing nature of Internet links, the Rosen Publishing
Group, Inc., has developed an online list of Web sites related to the
subject of this book. This site is updated regularly. Please use this
link to access the list:

http://www.rosenlinks.com/gttc/scbt

FOR FURTHER READING

Chafe, William Henry, ed., et al. *Remembering Jim Crow: African Americans Tell About Life in the Segregated South*. New York: New Press, 2001.

Hine, Darlene Clark. *The Path to Equality: From the Scottsboro Case to the Breaking of Baseball's Color Barrier* (Milestones in Black American History). Broomall, PA: Chelsea House Publishers, 1995.

Horne, Gerald. *Powell v. Alabama: The Scottsboro Boys and American Justice* (Historic Supreme Court Cases). Danbury, CT: Franklin Watts, Inc., 1997.

Lee, Andrew H., ed. *Scottsboro, Alabama: A Story in Linoleum Cuts*. New York: New York University Press, 2002.

Levine, Ellen. *Freedom's Children: Young Civil Rights Activists Tell Their Own Stories*. New York: Putnam Publishers Group JUV, 1993.

Rochelle, Belinda. *Words With Wings: A Treasury of African-American Poetry and Art*. New York: HarperCollins Juvenile Books, 2000.

Stein, R. Conrad. *The Great Depression* (Cornerstones of Freedom). New York: Children's Press, 1994.

BIBLIOGRAPHY

Carter, Dan T. *Scottsboro: A Tragedy of the American South*. Baton Rouge, LA: Louisiana State University Press, 1969.

Chalmers, Allan K. *They Shall Be Free*. Garden City, NY: Doubleday & Company, 1951.

Court TV Online. "The High Court Speaks." Retrieved July 9, 2002 (http://www.courttv.com/greatesttrials/scottsboro/powellvstate.html).

Court TV Online. "The Scottsboro Boys." Retrieved July 9, 2002 (http: www.courttv.com/greatesttrials).

Dunn, Adam. "The Scottsboro Boys: Nine Lives Overlooked, Lost." CNN.com. Retrieved July 9, 2002 (http://www.cnn.com/2001/SHOWBIZ/TV/04/02/scottsboro).

Goodman, James. *Stories of Scottsboro*. New York: Pantheon Books, 1994.

"The Great Depression in the United States." Microsoft Encarta Encyclopedia Standard, 2001.

Hughes, Langston. *The Collected Poems of Langston Hughes*. New York: Alfred A. Knopf, Inc., 1994.

Linder, Douglas O. "The Scottsboro Boy Trials." Retrieved June 24, 2002 (http://www.law.unkc.edu/faculty/projects/ftrials).

Noble, Mike. "Causes and Effects of the Great Depression." Retrieved July 24, 2002 (http://www.oasis.bellevue.k12.wa.us/sammamish/sstudies.dir/hist_docs.dir/grtdepression.mn.html).

PBS Online. "Scottsboro: An American Tragedy." Retrieved July 3, 2002 (http://www.pbs.org/wgbh/amex/scottsboro).

"Scottsboro Case." Microsoft Encarta Encyclopedia Standard, 2001.

Vassell, Olive, ed. "The Scottsboro Boys." Retrieved July 9, 2002 (http://www.afro.com/history/scott/scotts.html).

PRIMARY SOURCE IMAGE LIST

Cover: Photograph of Samuel Leibowitz with the Scottsboro Boys. Taken in 1933 in Decatur, Alabama.

Page 4: Photograph of the Scottsboro Boys. Taken on March 25, 1931, in Scottsboro, Alabama.

Page 8: Photograph of an unemployed man during the Great Depression. Taken circa 1929–1939 in the United States.

Page 9: Photograph of hobos riding a freight car. Taken on October 23, 1934, in California.

Page 10: Photograph of Victoria Price. Taken on April 1, 1933, in Decatur, Alabama.

Page 11: Photograph of Ruby Bates. Taken in New York City on May 3, 1933.

Page 13: Photograph of Victoria Price on the stand in Decatur, Alabama. Taken on April 4, 1933.

Page 14: Photograph of the Scottsboro, Alabama, courthouse. Taken on April 4, 1933.

Page 15: "Stop Lynching" button. Created and distributed by the NAACP. From the collection of David and Janice Frent.

Page 19: Photograph of trial spectators in Scottsboro, Alabama. Taken on April 6, 1931, by an Associated Press photographer.

Page 21: Photograph of Charlie Weems, taken on April 10, 1933, in Decatur, Alabama. Photograph of Clarence Norris, taken in Alabama in 1933.

Page 22: Photograph of Ozie Powell testifying in Decatur, Alabama, on April 7, 1933.

Page 24: Photograph of Dr. R. R. Bridges on the stand. Taken on April 3, 1933, in Decatur, Alabama.

Page 27: Drawing of the higher court as a vulture. Printed in 1931.

Page 28: Poster supporting the Scottsboro Boys, dating from 1931. Created by the Emergency Scottsboro Defense Committee in New York City.

Page 30: Photograph of Haywood Patterson in prison. Taken in December 1945, in Decatur, Alabama.

Page 33: Photograph of the Decatur, Alabama, courthouse. Taken on April 4, 1933.

Page 35: Photograph of Jack Tiller and Victoria Price. Taken in Decatur, Alabama, on November 29, 1933.

Page 36: Photograph of Lester Carter on the stand in Decatur, Alabama, on April 7, 1933.

Page 37: Photograph of Ruby Bates with mothers of the Scottsboro Boys. Taken on May 1, 1934, in New York City.

Page 38: Photograph of Judge James Horton. Taken in court in Decatur, Alabama, on April 4, 1933.

Page 41: Photograph of Samuel Leibowitz, Haywood Patterson, and George Chamlee. Taken on April 1, 1933, in Decatur, Alabama.

Page 43: Document showing expenditures incurred by the International Labor Defense in its legal defense of the Scottsboro Boys. April 11, 1931–August 1934. Housed in the Chicago Historical Society.

Page 45: Cartoon drawn by Burck. Printed in the *Daily Worker* on December 1, 1933.

Page 46: Photograph of Eugene Williams, Olen Montgomery, Samuel Leibowitz, Willie Roberson, and Roy Wright. Taken on July 26, 1937, in New York City.

INDEX

ABOUT THE AUTHOR

Lita Sorensen is a writer, designer, and artist living in Iowa City, Iowa, with her husband. She has published poetry, essays, and feature stories. This is her first book for young adults.

CREDITS

Cover, pp. 1, 4, 8, 9, 10, 11, 13, 14, 15, 21 (left), 22, 30, 33, 35, 36, 37, 38, 41, 46 © Bettmann/Corbis; pp. 19, 24 © AP/Wide World Photos; p. 21 (right) © Hulton-Deutsch Collection/Corbis; pp. 27, 28 © Hulton/Archive/Getty Images; pp. 43, 45 Chicago Historical Society.

Designer: Les Kanturek; **Editor:** Christine Poolos